From Darkness ...
to Light

A collection of poems, from my heart to yours

By Jason Delaney

From Darkness ... to Light

ISBN: 9798864957882
© Jason Delaney, October, 2023

All rights reserved. No part of this publication may be reproduced,
distributed, or transmitted in any form or by any means,
including photocopying, recording, or other electronic or mechanical methods,
without the prior written permission of the publisher,
except in the case of brief quotations embodied in critical reviews and
certain other non-commercial uses permitted by copyright law.
For permission requests, contact the publisher at the address below.

E-mail: jasedelaney@sky.com

Published independently by Robin Barratt
www.RobinBarratt.co.uk

TRIGGER WARNING!

The content herein focuses on the themes of mental health.

This book is dedicated to my beautiful wife and family who have encouraged me to put my words to paper and share the love. So this is for them, and you x.

ABOUT JASON

"I am 48 years old, with Irish ancestry, living in Wiltshire (UK) with my wife and four cats. I do not regard myself as a poet, but more an Emotional Lyricist. Due to the suicide of my best friend, and family loss, I have battled with my mental health, and often find it hard to express my emotions, but writing them down seems to cleanse my soul.

A few years ago, I was with my Granda when he passed away. My Da and I carried him out to the undertakers. I then went home and, at 3am and wrote my first poem, Irish Hero.

Both my GP, and my wife, feel I am Bipolar, but I feel that I am just an empath, and spend most days trying to help people find some happiness and joy in their lives. But when the darkness takes me ... I write in the hope that my words will resonate with like-minded people, and perhaps help them when their darkness comes.

Remember; never be afraid of the darkness - embrace the darkness, because you need to go through the darkness ... to get to the light."

Jason Delaney, October, 2023

Jason Delaney - Featured poet at *Poetry for Mental Health*.

CONTENTS

08.	Irish Hero
09.	I never went away
10.	I am always with you
11.	From darkness to light
12.	Today?
13.	The timeless ones
14.	Heaven's door
15.	Grief
16.	Halfway across the sky
17.	Butterfly
18.	Liquid emotion
19.	Senses
20.	Angelic whisper
21.	I walk by your side
22.	I haven't seen you for a while
23.	Empty chair
24.	Cool wind in his hair
25.	From whispers to a scream
26.	Silent screams
27.	The power of her smile
28.	Twenty years time
29.	The wife
30.	First light
31.	God took you home
32.	Through your veins
33.	Who said romance is dead?
34.	I'll always be here
35.	Drowning without water
36.	Time heals nothing
37.	Wisdom
38.	Perfect
39.	Suicide
40.	My heart belongs to you
41.	Under the winter moon
42.	Come to me
43.	If I could see you tomorrow
44.	Lost
45.	To my wife ...
46.	Broken smile
47.	My Da

48.	Red
49.	Casey
50.	It's OK to grieve
51.	Then I saw your face
52.	Man up they say!
54.	Colour blind
55.	Sausages
56.	The fight for normality
57.	Manchester twenty- two
58.	I am still here
59.	Two floors of mental health

From Darkness ... to Light

Irish Hero

Sometimes it's hard to know what to say,
When there are no words and the pictures are grey,
When life just stops, when loved ones depart,
A light goes out in the depths of your heart.

A hero to many and much loved by all,
Would give you his everything, catch when you fall,
Light up the room with a flash of his smile,
You ask for an inch; he'd give you a mile.

A family man who lived for his wife,
His kids and his grand kids, quite simply his life,
His strength was legend right up to the end,
How can all these broken hearts mend?

The spine of our family, the blood in my heart,
To say goodbye to him, where do you start?
It's hard to grieve when you know he's still here,
He's the light through the window, the wind in your ear.

He's the air that you're breathing, the warm when you're cold,
He's the kiss on your forehead, the hand that you hold,
He's the sound of your laughter, the stories you tell,
A picture of beauty, the chimes of a bell.

His name is Joe Delaney, a gentleman, the best,
This man hasn't left us, he's taking a rest,
Don't cry when you hear it, his name should be sung,
Joseph Delaney, our hero, forever young.

~

It's been a few years since my Granda went to sleep. I take solace in the fact that I was with him when he closed his eyes. My Da and I helped carry him into the undertaker's car at about 3am. Then I went home and wrote 'Irish Hero'. The hardest thing I ever did was read it at his funeral. But now I can read it and smile, because when I think of him I see his smile ... he had the best smile

I never went away
For those of you who are missing loved ones, take a walk with me ...

Walk with me through meadows, when you're missing me my love,
You'll tread the grass and think of me, I'll guide you from above,
The wind will brush you gently, you'll feel my presence near,
The sun will warm your grieving face and help to dry that tear.

There's nothing wrong with crying, it's natural to be sad,
Your tears are liquid memories of the times that we once had,
But let me reassure you, I am with you all the time,
My leaving you was God's wishes; your sadness is the crime.

Lift your head a little higher as we walk the dew drenched field,
My soul ensures your safety, it protects you like a shield,
If you look on to the distance, you'll see an old oak tree,
The branches wave a loved hello, they wave because of me.

Sit down by the tree now, and think of that last day,
My body was tired, it needed rest, but I never went away,
Right now, I'm sat beside you, I hear you talk to me,
I'm smiling as I listen, if only you could see.

Walk with me through the meadows, let's walk along the stream,
The water flows like memories when I meet you in your dream,
I want to say I love you and you'll see my face one day,
But rest assured I'm with you now, as I never went away.

I am always with you

I stood by your bed last night, I came to have a peep, I could see that you'd been crying, you found it hard to sleep.

I whispered to you softly as you brushed away a tear, "It's me, I haven't left you. I'm well. I'm fine. I'm here."

I was close to you at breakfast, I watched you pour the tea, You were thinking of the many times your hand reached out to me.

I was with you at the shops today, your arms were getting sore, I longed to take the weight from you, I wish I could do more.

I was with you at my grave today, you tend it with such care, I want to reassure you, that I'm not lying there.

I walked with you towards your house as you fumbled for your key, I gently put my hand on you, I smiled and said, "It's me."

You looked so very tired and sank into your chair, I tried so hard to let you know that I was standing there.

It's possible for me to be so near you every day, To say to you with certainty "I never went away."

You sat there very quietly, then smiled, I think you knew, That in the stillness of that evening, I was very close to you.

The day is over, I smile and watch you yawning, And say "Goodnight, I love you, I'll see you in the morning."

And when the time is right for you to cross the brief divide, I'll rush across to greet you and we will stand side by side.

I have so many things to show you, there are many things to see, Be patient ... live your life good ... then come home to be with me.

From darkness to light

Sometimes I would be so very down,
There's a smile on my face, my heart wore a frown,
I'd sit in a dark room, my head full of mist,
In that moment in time, I didn't exist.

That's all I wanted, the pain to subside,
You feel like the goodness inside you has died,
The world would be a happier place without me,
 That's all I would think, I just couldn't see.

They tell you to smile and all is OK,
That doesn't help me, I just want to say,
'I'm broken...please fix me... ' but I just don't,
I should ask for some help, but I know that I won't.

They say to love yourself and then things get well,
That's rubbish, who'd love me, my life is a hell,
I need someone to see as I see, to feel like I do,
To change the sad grey sky back to bright blue.

Then one day it happens, you meet that special one,
The one that ties you back together where once you'd come undone,
They see beyond the imperfections and fall in love with you,
They understand the pain inside as they were broken too.

Whenever I feel darkness, I head towards the light,
I go and kiss my Katie's face, she makes everything alright,
She helped me fight my demons, I do the same for her,
My life is in full focus now, before it was a blur.

I guess the message I'm sending, all be it not too clear,
Is maybe love is the cure for all dark things we fear,
The darkness never leaves you, it still exists inside,
I hide it with my love for others and stubborn Irish pride.

If I'm feeling sadness, like it's raining in my head,
I go and see a loved one, cos when all is done and said,
We all have our own demons, but never give up the fight,
It's only then that you move from the darkness, and start living in the light.

Today?

Today I got up, but I didn't feel right,
I was fine when I went to my bed last night,
Why do I feel like my heart is in pain?
Would it be OK if I went to sleep again?
I feel really funny, I'm not sure what's wrong,
Like in my life's music, there's no words in my song,
Like everyone likes me but I'm feeling quite lost,
Yesterday I was summer, today winter frost,
This can't be normal, what the fucks going on?
The happiness I felt yesterday seems to have gone,
But there's no fucking reason, how can this be?
I guess that's the price I pay for just being me ...

Today I got up with a smile on my face,
I feel really as happy and not in a bad place,
What was wrong with me yesterday, I felt really down,
I wanted to smile but woke up with a frown,
I must be a weirdo cos that's never right,
I'm either happy as sunshine or as lost as the night,
Life is good today as everything's clear,
I will go out and socialise, be happy and cheer,
People like me being happy, is that the real me?
How will I be feeling tomorrow? I'll have to wait and see ...

Today?

~

If you know someone like this, give them a great big hug and tell them that you are there if they need you ...

The timeless ones

When darkness takes me and I can feel no more,
When my doorway of life has closed its last door,
When my eyes cannot open as there is nothing to see,
The Timeless Ones give me the strength to be me.

When the fear of just living makes me feel weak,
When the pain makes my heart cry and redemption I seek,
When the day has just broken and I long for the night,
The Timeless Ones give me the strength to just fight.

When the sound of my laughter is distant and rare,
When the hope I once felt turned to despair,
When the memories of them play on in my mind,
The Timeless Ones give me the strength to be kind.

When I smile as I'm happy and the day seems so bright,
When I live for the day now not the solace of night,
When I can be happy and not shed a tear,
The Timeless Ones are present, I feel they are near.

When our loved ones lie resting and it hurts just to live,
Remember they are with you and this message I give,
They are with you forever, they live on somehow,
The Timeless Ones look after you, .they are with you right now.

Heaven's door

You never really lost me, only the body dies,
My soul is free from a broken shell now stop those silent cries,
I walk with you, I look after you and I do so with a smile,
I'm sure you feel my presence, maybe once in a while.

You see I am your life's shadow, a reflection of time gone by,
I'm even there when the lights go out, I'm a star up in the sky,
I wish I could take your sorrow, and set your laughter free,
I'm with you now, and forever more, one day you will see.

You keep looking at my pictures, a memory stuck in time,
To waste your life in sadness just has to be a crime,
If only I could tell you, if only you could know,
My soul just left my body, but I'll never let you go.

I sometimes think you feel me, when I gently hold your hand,
I feel that you are happy, and maybe understand,
That somewhere over that rainbow is heaven, please believe,
But I will always stay with you to help your broken heart grieve.

I'll stay with you till one day, your body's broken too,
You'll see me standing right there, right there next to you,
You'll take my hand, and we will hug, and you will cry no more,
As we will be together when we knock on heaven's door.

Grief

I'm OK. I'm fine. What is death? Just means I can't see them that's all. But I miss seeing them. I know they are still here. Or do I? Yes, you do. You feel them close. Then why do I feel sad? It's because you can't see them. I miss them. The sun seems colder. The wind smells strange. Don't be silly. What is death? Is it God punishing me? What have I done? Is it fair? No. It's life. I feel OK today. But I feel guilty for feeling ok. That's not right. I miss them. But they are still with me. What is death? Death is a bastard. I feel sad today, but the sun seems warmer than yesterday. I miss them. I wonder if they see me cry. I feel ok today. Gotta carry on. I'll pretend to be happy. What is death? It's something that takes the body away in order to leave the soul with us. Really? It makes things easier to think that way. I've got to smile today. I feel guilty smiling. It's ok to smile. It's a mask I will wear. The sun seems warmer today. The wind still smells strange. Why does everything remind me of them? Why? It's because you love them. You don't just stop loving them because you can't see them silly. I know. I smiled today. I even laughed. They say grief gets better after time. Really? Grief never leaves. You just learn how to live with it. It's not a choice that you have. The sun seems warmer today. The wind is making a strange sound though. Is that them talking to me? Don't be silly. Yes. I don't know. I'm OK. I'm fine. Aren't I ... ?

Halfway across the sky

Look up to the sky my love when dawn it starts to break,
When you realise you can't see me and your heart begins to ache,
For as the new days dawning, and the sun lights up your face,
The warmth you feel is my loving touch, you're feeling my embrace.

Look up to the sky my love when your face it wears a frown,
Our eyes will meet halfway as I'm always looking down,
You talk to me, I hear you, emotions leave your eye,
My body has gone, but I am here, our love will never die.

Look up to the sky my love and show me that great smile,
Our memories will give you strength, if only for a while,
I'm guiding you remember, I'm deep within your soul,
Your heart it may be broken, my spirit keeps it whole.

I want you to remember, that I am always here,
I say your name upon the breeze and whisper in your ear,
When time it has no meaning, and you let life just pass you by,
Look up my love, and we will meet, halfway across the sky ...

Butterfly
For my Nan, Fly high, Butterfly

Please do not mourn me for I am still here,
My body just grew weary so wipe away that tear,
I opened my eyes in heaven, there is no more pain,
My husband was there to greet me, and I can see my mother again.

The flowers here are wonderful, I have a garden too,
It's not as nice as my one back home but I'll see what I can do,
I feed the birds quite often, they visit me each day,
Dad wants to help me with the roses, but he'll just get in the way.

My legs are working fine now, they seem like they're brand new,
I've left behind my spectacles as my eyesight is good too,
I'm living in my happy times, and I don't want to see you cry,
It was my time; I chose to go so please don't question why.

My family are my everything and I'll stay by your side,
I know that you all love me, and it fills me up with pride,
I want you all to be strong now, you know I don't like tears,
Remember all those happy times we've had throughout the years.

I leave behind such sadness, but it was my decision to go,
Keep my memory close to your heart and I want you to know,
My life has been wonderful, but it was time for me to fly,
Like the graceful, beautiful butterflies that paint colour on the sky.

Liquid emotion

I remember the day when you breathed your last sigh,
I looked to the heavens, and I just asked why,
The church bells were ringing, they drowned out my cries,
That cold winter evening when God closed your eyes.

I walk past churches now just to hear the bells chime,
It eases the pain and somehow stops time,
I've accepted your gone but I feel you are near,
Your voice in the wind is a sound I still hear.

I know we will meet again somewhen somewhere,
That makes life without you easier to bear,
Until that day I will wear this happy disguise,
As the liquid emotions escape from my eyes…

Senses

I hear your voice through the wind in the trees,
Your whispers are on the cold winter breeze,
You talk to me when the church bells will ring,
It comforts me and it makes my heart sing.

I see your image in the rise of the morning sun,
The warmth on my face stops me coming undone,
It creates shadows of me, I know that is true,
But in my self-comforting mind, I hope that it's you.

I smell your scent as I breath in the air,
It somehow softens my inner despair,
I'll reminisce to a time we once had,
The tears they are happy, but sometimes are sad.

I often feel numb, and it rains in my head,
They say wine is for blood and the flesh is the bread,
I'm not sure that I believe in God up above,
But then he must exist as he gave me your love.

My senses will guide me, and you'll help me feel,
That I must carry on living, my life is real,
I'll live in your honour as I love you so much,
Those tears that escape me are your liquid touch.

Angelic whisper

I feel you near me, I just know your here,
And I often dream that you'll just reappear.

Yes, I know that you're home now, your work is done,
But it's your warmth I feel when I look at the sun.

I know you are watching me and guiding my mind,
You are the reason that I try to be kind.

I've learned not to be nasty and always be true,
And help others that are not as fortunate as you.

I know that your body has gone home to rest,
But your soul is still with me, it's deep in my chest.

I talk to you often, I know you can hear,
Sometimes I'm silent, my eyes speak with a tear.

Through loss comes changes, it's true what they say,
I changed into, I hope, a better man today.

You help me, I know it, I do understand,
I hope you're sat with me as I type with this hand.

I'll carry on walking life's path with a smile,
As I know you are with me and once in a while.

I'll hear your voice through the wind in the trees,
An angelic whisper carried on the breeze.

I walk by your side

I'm there when you wake as the sun breaks at dawn,
You open your eyes as a new day is born,
I watch as you wake up with your beating sad heart,
I know you can't see me but we're never apart.

I'm there when you leave home, to work you must go,
Your smile is your mask, so the sadness won't show,
I listen when you talk to me, you think I can't hear,
My reply is a whisper of wind in your ear.

I'm there when you're angry because you can't see me,
I wish you could know that you I can see,
I'd love to take all of your sadness away,
But you brave the days darkness and continue your day.

I'm there when you're happy as works nearly done,
You walk towards home, but you just want to run,
I see your emotions leave your eye in a tear -
I wish you could know that I am still here.

I'm there when you wait for the cruel day to end,
A broken heart is a thing that just won't mend,
You miss me, I know that and I miss you too,
I never left your side, I'm still with you.

I'm there when you go to bed, I help close your eyes,
You are with me again as the day slowly dies,
I watch as the dreams make you smile once again,
They seem to be the remedy to your heavy hearts pain.

If only you knew that I'm here with you now,
I'll never leave you, no way, no how,
I love you and miss you, you fill me with pride,
Every life step you take ... I walk by your side.

I haven't seen you for a while

I look outside my window, the dark night is here again,
I always took for the brightest star, it somehow eases pain,
I haven't seen you for a while, I miss your beautiful face,
Until that day when we meet again, the brightest star I'll chase.

I feel at ease in silence, I'll sit in a darkened room,
My mind replays our memories, my heart an empty tomb,
I haven't seen you for a while, since you closed your eyes that day,
They tell me that you're with God now, so I close my eyes and pray.

I talk to you quite often, I ask for your advice,
I want to be just like you, so wonderful and nice,
I haven't seen you for a while, but I'm trying hard to live,
I want to be a better man, I have so much love to give.

I wait for nights dark hours, when I can finally close my eyes,
I'll see you in my dreams again, this stops my souls' lost cries,
I haven't seen you for a while, but I know I will tonight,
You'll hold me tight and kiss my face and give me the strength to fight.

I look outside my window, the darkness turns to light,
I feel you with me, it helps me live without you in my sight,
I haven't seen you for a while, but I think I understand,
That whilst I walk my path in life, you will forever hold my hand.

Empty chair

The house seems so much darker, the sounds are somewhat grey,
The happiness of living left home with you that day,
The pictures still remind me that you were really there,
But all that I can see now is your favourite empty chair.

My whole life I have known you, but now you've gone away,
My memories are like movies, in my mind is where they play,
Life carries on regardless, they say it get easier to bear,
But they haven't been to my house and seen your empty chair.

I'm not sure I should move it, what if you're still here?
I know your body is laid to rest but is your soul and spirit near.
I make sure that it's nice and clean, it eases my despair,
To think that somehow you live on in your favourite empty chair.

They say that time's a healer, I'm not sure that it's true,
But everywhere I go in life my thoughts return to you,
My heart is always lonely, but I'm too lost to care,
I'll carry on just sitting here, in your once favourite empty chair.

Cool wind in his hair
Dedicated to my Uncle Chris ... a huge Eagles fan.

"I like to believe he's in the clouds, soaring like an Eagle, over a dark desert highway, cool wind in his hair ..."

When our loved ones are resting it just makes no sense,
Is it gods will? Or the end of the innocence,
Life will go on, but we don't know just how,
As everything is different now,
A boy of summer, Chris Thomas his name,
A snapshot of beauty held still in life's frame,
He always feels near us though it seems very far,
He's putting music on the jukebox in hotel California's bar,
He's takin' it easy and he is in no pain,
He's riding his Harley, life in the fast lane,
A bird of free spirit, an eagle of life,
Missed greatly by his family, his children and wife,
Life is cruel sometimes, but we cope with what's in it,
We can't let it pass us like a New York minute,
Chris lives on through music whether it's wrong or right,
We think of him if we smile today or if there's a heartache tonight,
He is always with us, wherever we roam,
Heaven needed music, God said I'm taking you home.

From whispers to a scream

Since when has darkness been my friend?
Since when is life better when light ends?
Since when has the night conquered the day?
I believe it's since you went away.

My once happy soul has succumbed to fear,
My once dry cheek is now damp with my tear,
My once content life is feeling bereft,
I've been this way since the day that you left.

Time is a healer they all say to me,
Time has no meaning when it's you I can't see,
It's your face I see when I close my eyes,
Time is no healer, it's all just lies.

The dark is my protection, my cape of despair,
Yet I take comfort just knowing you're there,
I live in the darkness of my own dream,
Where my once happy thoughts go from whispers to a scream.

Silent screams

In life I am happy most of the time and go about my day,
I smile and laugh as best I can, that changed when you went away.

We lose our loved ones, that is life, and everybody cries,
But nothing I do will stop the silent scream behind my eyes.

Nobody can hear it, but I know that it is there,
It's like being awake all by yourself in the darkest bad nightmare.

Is it cos I miss you? Or that you should be here?
The silent screams they call to me and only I can hear.

I know it's grief I'm feeling, and time will ease the pain,
But just one thing will stop it, to see your face again.

I look at all your pictures, I remember better days,
The silent screams are still with me, but a lesser volume plays.

They say time it is a healer, and to a degree this is true,
I live my life with my memories and thinking about you.

I have found a way to ease the pain and hush the silent screams,
I close my eyes, with my mind on your face, and meet you in my dreams.

The power of her smile
I love my wife ...

Time it passes by so fast with beauty and with grace,
I never really noticed this until I saw her face,
I think I just existed, was just one of life's sighs,
But then I found that I was loved, she told me with her eyes,
It changed the way I feel inside about every single thing,
I can see where the rainbows end, I hear what the birds sing,
The thought of her makes me happy, it's written on my face,
My heart beats fast when near her, like its winning life's love race,
I understand what love is, I know now what it means,
It's how you feel when life is better than your dreams,

I now walk life's path happy, mile after mile,
And what has made me feel this way?
the power of her smile x

Twenty years time
For my Katie x

I live for the moment, that much is true,
But when I think of the future ... I see you,
The summers are hotter and the winters much colder,
You will still be beautiful in my eyes, just a little bit older.

In twenty years', time we'll still be in love,
My hand will fit yours like a custom made glove,
We'll frisk and we'll frolic, and we'll go out and play,
Just a little bit slower than we do today.

In twenty years', time I'll still hold you tight,
When the dreams become bad in the dark of the night,
I'll hug and I'll kiss you and remove all your fear,
You'll never be afraid as long as I'm near.

In twenty years' time we'll still be a team,
Our lives have become one in life's lushest dream,
I'll look after you and you'll look after me,
We'll be together with our beautiful family.

In twenty years' time you'll still own my heart,
It won't beat as strong as it did at the start,
A once wild heart, it took you to tame,
The beat from inside it spells out your name.

In twenty years' time we will feel the same,
You'll meet an old friend who will mention my name,
He'll ask, "Tell me what happened to that crazy chap Jase?",
You'll say "He's waiting for me to come home so he can kiss my face ..."

The wife
Princess Katie x

To hear your heart beating as I lay on your chest,
Is my favourite sound, in fact, it's the best,
Your sleeping pretty face as I wake at dawns break,
Holds more beauty than a sculpture could ever make,
Your smile when you see me makes everything ok,
It makes me feel colour where once just was grey,
The sparkle your eyes show when happiness takes hold,
Is prettier than diamonds, more value than gold,
The warmth of your touch as your hand holds my hand,
Makes me feel love, I finally understand,
That it's you pretty princess that makes my heartbeat,
My essence, my lifeline, you make me complete,
Thank you for loving me, I know it's hard work,
I can be a grumpy, yet damn handsome burk,
Believe when I tell you, that God made a plan,
To make bacon delicious, and make me your man.

First light

Darkness is present, it's all I can feel, until the first light, then the day becomes real.

Morning has broken, a new day is born, I'm broken too, my soul it is torn.

Black becomes grey, then light colours sky, I have to get up now, but I don't really know why.

Must I leave darkness? Am I safe in the light?

Every morning I feel this, it's anxiety I fight.

The sun it is rising, new shadows appear, the warmth of the new day, it fills me with fear.

I look through my window, the birds are in song, the world seems alright, yet I feel so wrong,

I'm scared of the living, and miss those who are dead, if my life was a story, this chapters unread.

Why am I like this? This is not right ... I belong in the darkness; I fear that first light.

God took you home

I often think of your face when I wake upon a day,
The smile you wore was made of gold, it's never gone away,
I write these rhymes to mourn you, it's the only way I know,
don't be cross if I feel sad, I love you still you know.

I wish I'd spent more time with you before you went away,
It's not good to regret in life but I feel this every day,
I know you look upon me from the beauty of the stars,
You wipe my tears when I'm upset and heal my emotional scars.

I knew that you were poorly but never thought you'd go,
To me you were indestructible, how little did I know,
I understand it was time to leave but that doesn't make it right,
I see your face every single day and hear your voice at night.

In tears I saw you sinking, I watched you fade away,
My heart was almost broken, I wanted you to stay,
But when I saw you sleeping, so peaceful, free from pain,
How could I wish you back with us, to suffer once again.

I love and miss you dearly, I write this with a tear,
I'm happy that you're at peace now, but wish you were still here,
It broke my heart to lose you, but you did not go alone,
For part of me went with you .. .the day God took you home.

Through your veins

The world has stopped turning, the sun is now cold,
The wind smells of sadness, my life is on hold,
I heard that you'd left us, no word of goodbye,
I sit in the darkness, and I start to cry.

Why did you do it? You should have called me,
Could I have saved you? Could I make you see?
I know you had troubles, why didn't you share?
I'm openly sobbing, it's just not fair.

The last time I saw you, we had a fight,
Now I can't say sorry, I can't make things right,
You've left me feeling guilty, I feel so bad,
You were the best friend that I've ever had.

I'm still in the darkness, I'm drowning in grief,
Why should I face the world when it gives no relief,
I wish you were still here, I wish I was not,
Maybe I'll go with you, I may give it a shot.

But I don't have the courage to take my own life,
I can't leave my family, I can't leave my wife,
Is it courage you needed to extinguish your flame?
I am not brave enough to leave so much pain.

The needle in your arm shot solace to your heart,
It also broke mine as I fall apart,
I'll stay in the darkness, I'll stay on the ground,
Where I'll still ask you why, as I cry without sound.

Who said romance is dead?

Hello there wife here's a poem for you,
Ferrets they bite and pigeons go coo,
I could send you flowers, some do to their birds,
But you will be gifted with these golden words.

This isn't a sorry, I've done nothing wrong,
You are in my mind, like the words of a song,
It's like you are the music, and I am the rhyme,
When brought together, irrelevant is time.

I happen to think you're a nice piece of fluff,
You are the beauty queen, and I'm your bit of rough,
These words are immortal, and flowers would die,
Is an apple crumble better than a pie?

Sorry got distracted, that happens to me,
Maybe it's time to get all soppy,
Your hair is autumn fall, your eyes are emotions peak,
You're so Flippin tasty, like the burger I had last week.

Or maybe before I met you is hard to remember,
My branches were bare like the trees in December,
You warm up my soul with the warmth of your heart,
When we said I do to the vicar lady, our story did start.

Blimey that's good, I bet you're impressed,
I'd normally say can I play honk with your chest,
Maybe flowers would be better, I don't really know,
I'll finish this ode off, it is worth a go.

I hope you are smiling and filled up with joy,
I'm very pleased that you are my girl, and I am your boy,
Whoever said romance was dead has not met me,
So Katie, I love you ... and what's for tea?

I'll always be here
This is for those of you who cannot see their Ma today.

I know that you miss me, your tears tell me so,
But I really am fine, and I want you to know,
Although you can't see me or my voice you can't hear,
Take comfort in the fact that I am still here.
I'm there when you're happy, I'm there when you're mad,
I'm smiling when you smile, I hug you when you're sad,
No matter what the occasion, I want to be clear,
I'm the breath in your lungs, I am still here.
I watch while you're sleeping, I'm there when you wake,
I guide your actions with every life step you take,
I'll guide you and protect you so please never fear,
For I am your angel, I am still here.
I hear when you talk to me, and I miss you too,
I talk to you back, I'm so proud of you,
Wherever your life takes you, I will be near,
I'll be holding your hand; I am still here.
I'm sat with you now, through your eyes I see,
My only wish is for you to be happy,
So please go have fun, laugh, and cheer,
I am your shadow. I'll always be here.

Drowning without water

Life can be like the darkest ocean, so cold where the light shines dim,
Some people feel like they are treading water as they've forgotten how to swim,

Just peace is all these people want but there is never a reprieve,
To feel depressed is like drowning without water whilst those around you breathe.

Keep an eye out for these lonely folk for trust me they are near,
It's not always the quiet ones who are full of dread and fear,

Some hide their pain with laughter, and always wear a smile,
But the dark clouds hit all of us every once in a while.

It's important to be supportive of people in this pain,
They find it hard to feel the sun when their head is full of rain,

Hold their hand, comfort them or simply just be there,
Then those who drown without water can come up for some air.

Time heals nothing

I remember seeing you smile, I wish I could again,
Life was so much simpler, and things were different then,
You seemed to make life better, you'd make the bad things good,
I'd love to see you again, if only I could.

You weren't supposed to leave me, I still don't understand,
I still hear your last breath as I held your hand,
Deep down I know it was your time rest,
But why does the Lord above take the very best?

I sometimes hear you laughing, a whisper in the air,
It makes me feel happy, gives me the smile that I wear,
I know that you're at peace now, there will be no more pain,
But I'd sell my soul twice just to see you again.

They say time is a healer, I'm not sure this is true,
I'm not injured or damaged, I just really miss you,
Your smile was the greatest thing I ever saw,
It'll stay in my memory ... until I see you once more.

Wisdom

I think a lot ...

Being a little bit damaged makes you see the world in a different way ...

You notice the things normal folk don't.
You notice the faint scares on people's arms.
The emptiness in their eyes.
The way they smile with their mouths, not with their eyes.
The anxiousness they feel while eating in front of others.

Just little things that most would look over.

But you notice.

Because they're just like you ...

When you choose to love someone who is damaged you take on the weight of their past, their pain and their guilt.

You must be strong.
You must be patient.

You can stop the bleeding, and help them heal over.

But they will always be a little bit broken.

If you can handle that.
If you can accept the dents and the cracks.
If you can get them to trust you.
You will never find a more loving person than one who is damaged.
Above all else they know about survival.
After all ... they are still here.
Wondering if someone like you will ever love them.

Perfect

As we get older some things they have changed, The waistband gets bigger, your husband more deranged,

I know that you worry, your body is not the same, As the day when God blessed me and gave you my last name.

Trust me when I tell you, I do not love you less, You look as perfect today as you did in that dress,

Time takes its toll on our bodies that is true, Your beauty still remains, and I love you.

We all have some worries as flesh starts to squidge, We all plan our diets as we stare in the fridge,

Worry less about dress sizes as your beauty's intact,
I'm not telling a fib here; I'm stating a fact.

I have a dad bod, which I'm trying to toughen, Yet we both know I'm an Irish Stud Muffin,

Embrace what you are then life will be fun, I'd butter your muffin if you'll pardon the pun.

We should all just be happy, if we're chunky or thin,
Call the scales a bastard and throw it in the bin,

Have fun, enjoy life, while we still can,
You are just as beautiful now a the day you got in the fucking van.

Suicide

Darkness is like a pool of water.
We all feel darkness sometimes.
But that's just dipping your foot in the water.
Suicide ...you are fully immersed.
If any of you are ever any more than knee deep ...talk to someone.
Anyone.
Talk to me if you want.
Who cares if one more light goes out?
Well, I do ...

My heart belongs to you
A little ode I wrote for my wife at the beginning of our life journey

I look at you sometimes and I just think 'wow', This girl is my girlfriend, I just don't know how, That someone so special could ever love me, You don't think you're beautiful, you don't see what I see.

If God was an artist, it's your face he'd draw,
If your voice was his music, you'd want to hear more,
Your smile lights the room up, your heart it is pure,
 My heart was once lonely, but you were the cure.

I want to be the best boyfriend, but I know I am not,
I'm a rough assed Irishman and you are damn hot,
I want to be a better man and you help that be,
So thank you Katie Bennett, thank you for choosing me.

We have our little family and I love the way we are,
We both are massive geeks and zombies go raaaaggghhh,
I'm waffling now but this much is true,
Thank you for loving me, my heart belongs to you.

Under the winter moon

The winter it has fallen, the air is cold and grey,
I look up to the moon above as dusk rinses the light away,
Majestic stars surround it, on a canvas of eternal time,
I whisper that I miss you, a silent love filled mime.

Time it has no meaning, not without you by my side,
Some days are filled with laughter, and others I have cried,
The winter moon sends comfort, I have no idea why,
As we mourn the loss of loved ones gone, the moon will never die.

Under the winter moon we meet, just us, just you and me,
Where the coldness numbs the pain, and our hearts are once more free,
Our love is my eternal book, my memories are the pages,
Your light it helps to ease the pain, as it has throughout the ages.

Come to me

You know I miss your company and I cannot see you now,
But I know that you can see me, that comforts me somehow,
You're the warmth the sun shines brightly, the wind that's in the tree,
I want to know you're happy, in my dreams.

Please come to me.

I see the world is aging and all my loved ones too,
Time it has no meaning when I stop to talk to you,
I sometimes ask you questions, with my eyes closed on one knee,
I follow no religion, I follow you.

Please come to me.

I want to tell you how I feel and how I want you near,
A memory slides down my face in the capsule of a tear,
I know that you'd be angry, but I miss you bad you see,
So please, in dreams, however you can.

Please just come to me.

If I could see you tomorrow
(Where there is dark, there will always be light ... you just have to find it)

If I could see you tomorrow, I'd never let go of your hand,
We'd walk through our fields of memories, and I'd ask God to please understand,
My eyes on your face would heal me, as since you left, I have been sad,
My heart cried too when you left me and everything good turned to bad.

If I could see you tomorrow, I'd tape every word that you say,
My mind would be the recorder, And I'd play your words back every day,
We'd talk about how much I miss you, and you'd say that I'm always here,
You'd tell me that you, never left and it's true, that I have nothing to fear.

As time goes by things get better, they say so, but it's not true,
I'd walk through the flame, just to see you again, what the hell is my heart gonna do.

If I could see you tomorrow, I'd ask you to stay by my side,
We could just be together, I'm alone since the day that you died,
Do you hear when I cry, do you understand why, my heart it no longer sings,
I still hear your voice, be it memory or choice, when the beautiful church bell rings.

As time goes by things get better,
they say so, but it's not true,
I'd walk through the flame, just to see you again, what the hell is my heart gonna do.

If I could see you tomorrow, I'd ask you to come back again,
Stay with me now and forever, the only known cure for this pain, I'm surviving on your memories, and I want you to know,
I long for the day when I see you, I'll hold you and never let go.

As time goes by things get better,
they say so, but it's not true,
I'd walk through the flame, just to see you again, what the hell is my heart gonna do.

Lost

Why say be happy when I often feel sad?
Why try to be good when my soul says I'm bad?
Why say cheer up when my face shows my pain?
When will my heart be happy again?

I see life so clearly through tear filtered eyes,
I wear my fun mask, it's my only disguise,
I'm surrounded by loved ones, even ones I can't see,
So why does my mind keep punishing me?

Why is there darkness in a day full of light?
I feel I am losing my sanity fight,
I want to laugh, feel happy, feel the warmth of the sun,
Why do I feel that I'm coming undone?

I know there is good somewhere inside,
They said I'm a good man, I feel that they lied,
They say love yourself and all else will follow,
So why does my soul feel empty and hollow?

My mind is a dark place, who'd want to live there?
Am I living the dream, or some fucked up nightmare?
I should make an effort cos times running out,
All life is a risk so why do I doubt?

I helped someone today who was in a dark place,
There are others like me, I could see in their face,
I made someone smile and that made me feel good,
Can I make others happy? Maybe I could.

My mind is much lighter now but is often grey,
I get up each morning and take on the day,
I still find it hard to like being me,
But I don't care if I make others happy.

So now life is different, I try to be nice,
I help people who need it but what is the price?
It's free and it helps me, there is no cost,
To feel I have value stops me feeling lost.

To my wife ...

It's hard to love somebody when you don't much like yourself,
You walk lonely through life's journey content with being on the shelf,
Then you meet someone who loves you but it's hard to understand,
They want to walk life's path with you, and to hold your hand.

You make sense of my madness, and you love me for who I am,
You save me from sadness when the worries breach my minds dam,
You are my saviour, and I will always look after you,
A once lost soul you have grounded with a love that feels brand new.

I know I'm far from perfect, but you love me just the same,
To prove it to me and complete my life, you even took my name,
There are no words to tell you how proud I am that you're mine,
We'll walk this life together, with our babies, and that's just fine.

I've never understood emotions, my mind would always doubt,
Why don't people see the danger when you have your heart held out?
They're only going to hurt you, so why would you even try?
But then you gave me your heart, and finally, I understand why.

To summarise this ode of love, I want to say thank you,
I'm still an insane yet pant dampeningly handsome Irish bastard, but what you gonna do?!
My life is now in colour, before you it was grey,
I am yours, and you are mine, until my dying day.

I hope you like this poem, these soppy words are yours,
But now I must remind you, to go do your womanly chores,
Hopefully you are smiling, as you read this as you wake,
But now is the time to rise and shine for its breakfast you must make.

Love you Princess xx

Broken smile

I hate when I see no smile their face,
When friends are down and in a dark place,
I've been there you see and I'm not going back,
So I help these lost souls get back on life's track,
We all are so different but inside the same,
Our emotions are wild and so hard to tame,
We all have certain friends who struggle in life,
Could be your best pal, your husband, your family or wife,
Asking for help is a hard thing to do,
When you simply don't know what is wrong with you,
You want to punch life with your own clenched fist,
And you pray to a god that just doesn't exist,
But out of darkness comes light and happiness too,
I am the proof, believe me it's true,
Take care of your friends, go that extra mile,
Look out for the ones with the broken smile.

My Da

I'm not very good when it comes to emotions,
I just hide my thoughts and go through the motions,
It makes things seem better and it hides the pain,
But it makes your heart cold and your mind full of rain.

My Da always told me to talk to him more,
But I don't like talking, I don't want to bore,
But he's clever my Da, he gets in my head,
Before I know it, everything's been said.

As a kid I was horrid but my Da was always there,
I'd be in fights and trouble, but he would always be fair,
If I was over my head he was there to protect,
It is from him that I learned to respect.

We all love our Da's but mine is my mate,
The man's full of kindness and empty of hate,
If I'm half the man that my Da turned out to be,
I'd just kiss that man's face and die happy.

Love you Da x

Red

You were 14 when we said goodbye,
Time to chase those rainbows in the sky,
It's been four years since that painful day,
But the sadness, it won't go away.

You were my boy, my little man, you were my son,
The day that you left me my life came undone,
I talk to you daily, I'll never forget,
You were the most wonderful boy that I've ever met.

You are my son and I miss you and you'll always be mine,
They say times a healer, but I'll never be fine,
I know you are happy and live in my dreams,
It's you that I think of when my smiles at full beam.

You are my little angel, my star in the sky,
I know you're at peace now, so I've stopped asking why,
I miss your face dearly and although we're apart,
Your paw prints can be found, in the depths of my heart.

Casey

I was getting a cat, never had one before,
The door opened, I looked down at the floor,
I remember you walked in on your little paws,
Our eyes met, you head bumped me, right then I was yours.

You were a tiny little kitten, but you were the boss,
I'd get a good hiding if you ever got cross,
A force to be reckoned with, but cute just the same,
I called you Casey and gave you my last name.

Through all of my tough times you've been by my side,
Calmed me down if I'm angry, licked my tears if I've cried,
You knew when I felt sadness, you'd lay on my chest,
Your heart melting purrs lay my worries to rest.

When your health started falling, not once were there moans,
Your heart it was failing, and you had aches in your bones,
You fought on, my warrior, my beautiful one,
I'd carry you everywhere, your legs couldn't run.

I know you weren't suffering, you'd just gotten old,
When God made my girl, he then broke the mould,
You slept by my feet, and I'd bring you breakfast in bed,
Then I'd hold you in your litter tray whilst stroking your head.

I held your paw when you breathed your last sigh,
And I'm so not ashamed to say I started to cry,
My daughter has left me, this cannot be real.
There are simply no words to say how I feel.

Your Papa adored you and still does right now,
I looked after you good, the best I knew how,
Thank you for loving me and making me yours,
I miss those pretty eyes and beans on your paws.

As hurt as I am I know it was right,
But I'll see you again when I dream at night,
I know you are with me; I keep finding fur,
And through the wind in the trees, I still hear you purr ...

It's OK to grieve

We all deal with grief in our own special way,
But when people say 'get over it' that's just not OK,
There isn't a time limit, grief is always there,
It's a silent scream inside you that tells you that you care.

You'd think that it gets easier, and time would be reprieve,
But every time I think of you it's suddenly harder to breathe,
The pain is my soul's memory, a reminder that we're apart,
Your life was so important to me, you're leaving tore my heart.

Sometimes I get angry and want to just scream,
I just want to close my eyes to see you in my dream,
I listen as the wind blows now, it doesn't sound the same,
But I take comfort in the fact that it does call out your name ...

Then I saw your face

I would wonder through life's highways, I would always feel alone,
I'd see the world was happy, it cut me to the bone,
For I was broken inside, my smile has gone away,
I wanted heart salvation, I longed for it one day.

Then I saw your face,
My life now had a meaning ...

Then I saw your face,
I must be surely dreaming ...

I wake up in the morning, what is real or dream,
Reality is blurred now, things are not what they seem,
How can I be happy, when I'm broken up inside, I long for new
beginnings and break the shackles of this pride.

Then I saw your face,
My life now had a meaning ...

Then I saw your face,
I must be surely dreaming ...

You make me feel alive now, my lover and my friend,
Life is so much better knowing I'm with you till the end,
For the broken parts are healed now, my heart it beats your name,
The sun is so much brighter, and I'm winning life's love game.

As I see your face,
My life it now has meaning ...

And I love your face,
I think I must be dreaming ...

Then I see your face,
When I wake up each morning ...

And I love your face,.
I know that I'm not dreaming ...

Man up they say!

Three quarters of suicides are male.

Did you know that?

The biggest killer in men before they reach the age of 50 is their own mind?

Not heart attacks or cancer.

"Man up!" they say. "You're a man. Fucking act like one"

And there lies one of the issues ...

It isn't manly to talk about worries.
It isn't manly to discuss feeling depressed.
It isn't manly to think you may have mental health issues.
It isn't manly not being able to cope.

Is this generational? Or Cultural even? Both I'd say yet in this modern world it still exists.

They say men should "talk more" and whilst this is true, for some it is not so easy.

Some men hide it well.

Think of it like this ... The thing about broken clocks is you can always tell exactly when they stopped ticking.

With people it isn't so easy.

And sometimes you can't even tell they are broken...

Of course, this is not limited to men, but the suicide statistics speak for themselves.

It is encouraging that this is being addressed now and more men are opening up.

So, fuck this "Man up" mentality, culture or whatever the fuck it is ...

Everyone has probably been affected by suicide. I lost my best mate.
However, I still find it hard to talk. I write it down instead.
It kinda purges me.

But I know that if I need anyone to talk to ... they are there.
And sometimes that is enough.

I will always be here for anyone who needs advice, an ear ...
or whatever ...

Men have to realise that they don't have to man up ... *to prevent another man down.*

Colour blind

In a world that is so diverse, it saddens me to see,
The ugly face of racism staring right at me,
Why are people judged by the colour of their skin?
Such ignorance is rampant in this world that we live in.

Your skin's a certain colour, what difference does that make?
Some people try to change their own with colours that are fake,
I often see a spray tanned face, blended with a smudge,
It is their own choice to look that way and who am I to judge?

I don't understand the cruelty, evil has a name,
Racism is an ignorant sin, underneath we're all the same.
As humans we are so flawed, society needs to mend,
I don't care what colour you are, I will be your friend.

I see the different colours, and yet I see right through,
I don't judge on pigmentation, and neither should you,
I wish for some acceptance, where people are just kind,
The world would be a better place, and like me … be colour blind

~

There is a lot of racism in the news right now … I don't understand how humans get things so wrong sometimes, judging people by their skin colour … makes me cross … grrrr … see I turned my thoughts into a poem …

Sausages

'Ello there Wife this poem's for you,
It isn't recycled no it's brand new,
I thought I'd write a rhyme to make you giggle, It should make you dance and give that ass a wiggle,
Do you think sausages sometimes speak French?
Or do they watch cricket on an old park bench?
Do they throw flannels at a librarian called Sam?
Is their favourite doughnut a custard or jam?
Do they watch *Eastenders* or *Emmerdale* Farm?
Are they real confident or do they self-harm?
Do they wear trainers, or do they wear shoes?
Do they like rock music or rhythm and blues?
These are questions we need to address,
It is time to learn more as right now we know less,
Sausages are mysterious and maybe tonight,
We should buy some and do what is right,
Ask them these questions, let's give it a bash,
And if they stay silent, let's eat them with mash.

The fight for normality

It's morning again, I hate how night flies,
In darkness I'm safe, don't want to open my eyes,
In dreams I am normal, I have worth, I am real,
In the cold light of day this is not how I feel.

Would anyone notice if I'm no longer here?
Would the people that know me even shed a tear?
I don't think they would as I feel like a freak,
I'm worthless, I'm nothing, I'm empty and weak.

The smile on my face is a mask full of lies,
Who could respect a grown man that cries,
I hide behind laughter when the darkness it creeps,
Through the depths of my mind as my soul gently weeps.

Normality's a myth, it's not there to find,
It's hard to have friends when the enemy's your mind,
Why must I feel that everything is wrong?
I will even find darkness to the lyrics of song.

They say 'just be happy' but they just don't see,
That the problem with my life is because I am me,
I walk on through life just praying for that day,
When I feel I have purpose, and the pain goes away.

Manchester twenty- two

It's times like these I worry about the evil that lives here, Twenty-two lives lost and a nation sheds a tear, A disillusioned soul causes carnage for his belief, An act of utter madness, causes nothing except mass grief.

It's times like these I wonder if religion is even right, If it isn't in the equation, would we even need to fight? No God would ask for killing, if you think so you are wrong, Life is far too precious, it's the lyrics to Gods own song.

It's times like these I shed a tear for the families left behind, And the beautiful folk that help them with hearts that are just kind, The evil around us is growing but it will never win, There is no place in heaven for a soul that full of sin.

It's times like these I'm angry that hatred has a name, Terrorism is the label, but it's evil just the same, There simply is no God above that would justify this act, We need to destroy these evil folk with no mercy and that's a fact.

It's times like these I'm confident that they will never win, These acts of evil are pointless and to any god a sin, We will hunt you; we will find you, and as sure as time will tell, You will be punished, in the name of God, and burn in the depths of hell.

It's times like these I'm proud of the nation where we stand, We mourn right now for the losses, yet we just don't understand, If your religion asks you to take a life then please start and end with you, We shed a tear; we light a candle for the Manchester Twenty Two.

I am still here

I know that you miss me, your tears tell me so, But I really am fine, and I want you to know, Although you can't see me or my voice you can't hear, Take comfort in the fact that I am still here.

I'm there when you're happy, I'm there when you're mad, I'm smiling when you smile, I hug you when you're sad,No matter what the occasion, I want to be clear, I'm the breath in your lungs, I am still here.

I watch while you're sleeping, I'm there when you wake, I guide your actions with every life step you take, I'll guide you and protect you so please never fear, For I am your angel, I am still here.

I hear when you talk to me, and I miss you too, I talk to you back, I'm so proud of you, Wherever your life takes you, I will be near, I'll be holding your hand; I am still here.

I'm sat with you now, through your eyes I see, My only wish is for you to be happy, So please go have fun, laugh, and cheer, I am your shadow. I'll always be here

Two floors of mental health

There are two floors in my building,
This building is my mind,
Sometimes I don't know where I am,
My mental health's declined.

I am still the same old person,
That you have always known,
Yet the loud outgoing social chap can often feel alone.

The upstairs floor is awesome, full of life and happy times,
but downstairs is a cavern, it's dark and always blinds.

I want to have another floor, an emotional middle ground,
This would make me normal right? Normal has not been found.

There are two floors in my building,
I just go up and down,
I'll show you which floor I'm on with a nice smile or a frown,
But one thing is for certain, please remember I'm still me,
I have two floors in this building when most people will have three.

END

Printed in Great Britain
by Amazon